Violence
and the Secular

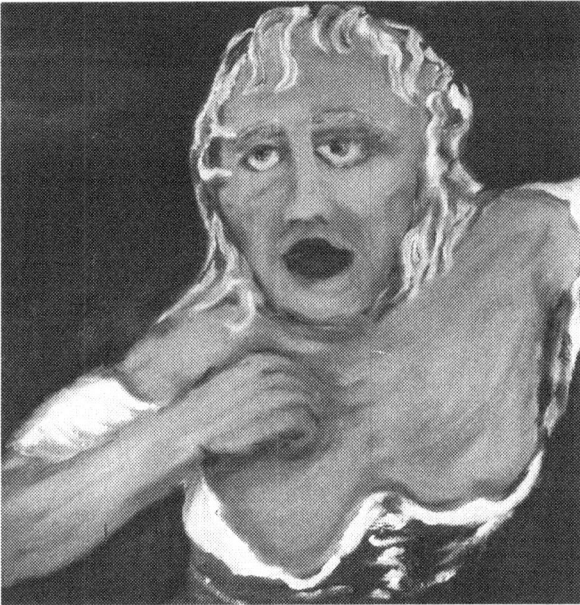

Douglas Canfield

Plain View Press
P. O. 42255
Austin, TX 78704

plainviewpress.net
sbright1@austin.rr.com
512-440-7139

For my daughters
Mary and Moriah

Contents

Prologue   7

Red Skies over Iraq   9

Various Violence 11

Violence and the Secular 13
Blown Away   14
Dantesque Blood   16
Our Gang   18
Pedophilia Catholica   20
Dark Night of the Soul   22
Domestic Violence   23
Ménage-à-trois   25
Professional Violence: The Agora   27
When Will They Ever Learn   28
Turkey Hunt   30
For Nicole Brown Simpson   33

Various Voices of Violence   35

Rape's Revenge   37
Don Juan 38
Doc   39
Shootout   40
Geronimo Speaks   41
Chato's Lament   42

Ballads from Hell   45

The Sisyphus Rock   47
Hang On, Ixion   49
Chin Up, Tantalus   51
The Prometheus Stone   52
Don't You Feel Like a Heel, Achilles   54

Recent Thunderings and Whisperings 55

Terrorism   57
Men of the Millenium   58
D. C. Revisited   59
Les Oiseaux du printemps   62
On Tampa Bay   63
Out West   65

The Shadow Knows 67

At Peace   69
Stowaway   70
For Taylor   71
Who Needs Kavorkian   72
The New Haven Green   73
The Medium Is the Message   74
Aurora   76
Florence   77
Je veux dire   78
The North Oregon Coast, Summer '02   79
Breathless   80

Epilogue 81

Barry Bonds's 73rd83

Prologue

Red Skies over Iraq

Mother Courage sniffs it on the wind.
Her Chaplain was right: peace doesn't last long,
It's the holes in the Swiss cheese of war.
Dryden wrote about his own saeculum saeculorum,
"Peace the lazy God has fled, Mars has looked the sky to red."
And the sky is red again over Baghdad.

I weep for the children of Iraq.
I weep for the "coalition" soldiers,
Young enough to be my grandchildren.
Mostly I weep for the ideals of my country,
Betrayed by an illegitimate junta,
Unelected by the people,
Emboldened by Big Money and Big Oil,
Contemptuous of social needs
And social justice.
Can't afford democracy both at home and in Iraq,
Don't you know?

Women flee the pursuing red, screaming,
Retreading the footsteps of similar refugees
From when the Assyrians first came down upon the fold,
When Alexander chased them to the Indus,
When Ventidius scattered the back-biting Parthians before him,
When Mahomet released his jihad hordes.

And now it's our turn? Shades of Mussolini into Ethiopia.
WE want a colony in the region.
The Manifest Destiny of the world's only righteous regime
Calls us again to venture forth. "Fools rush in —"
That was Pope, another poet intruding into my poem.
Because this is déjà vu all over again,
And my lament takes refuge in allusion and cliché.
Because who can find the words to make

Continued, no stanza break

The starkness of this reality stand out in bas relief
So we are all shocked and awed
At the awful arrogance of power?

Like Brecht's Kattrina,
One must risk beating the drum of warning.
Voices cry out in the wilderness,
Lighting candles around the globe.
They cannot snuff us all.

Various Violence

Violence and the Secular

Girard said sacred but meant
Secular, because the oversoul
Is *dead*, man, and violence
Is endemic to the planet,
Just ask your everyday tiger shark
Or your white-blood cells, man.

Religion itself has produced
Some pretty nasty rituals of its own:
Just ask the Aztecs or check it out
With Torquimado or empathize with
Recipients of teenage circumcision,
Female as well as male. Ouch.

Who're the best at torture?
Chinese, Japanese, Apaches?
Or those South American generals
We supported? Just ask Timerman,
And while you're at it, ask him
What he thinks of Teflon Pinochet.
Hey, we Europeans can hold our own, man.

Blown Away

We blew it, man.
So Peter Fonda tells Dennis Hopper
At the end of *Easy Rider*,
So says Charlton Heston
At the end of *Planet of the Apes*.

Paul Shepherd says we blew it
When we left the life-way of hunters
And started growing corn.

Buddha says we blew it
When we invented the self.

My wife says we blew it
When we invented patriarchs.

Did we blow it in the 1960s
When we dropped out and turned on?

Did we blow it in the 1860s
When we relinquished control to the machine?

Did we blow it when India and Pakistan,
Relinquishing any claim to moral leadership,
Joined the nuclear club?

What price civilization?
What price Bach and Shakespeare,
Borges, Picasso, Lao Tzu?

The city-builders gave us Paris,
Buenos Aires and Beijing
(Not to mention Chaco Canyon).

The meaning-makers gave us myth,
Religion, philosophy and art
And even Chaos Theory.

Has it been worth it at the price:
The virtual destruction of an ecosystem?

Where do we go from here?
Do we ride like Taylor
Back into our past
And start again?

Or will there be any of us left,
Not blown off the motorcycles of progress?

Dantesque Blood

Dante: a name evocative of lyrical satire,
Of metaphoric tries to capture the ineffable,
As the multifoliate rose unfolds before our eyes.

And yet another Dante clouds the view,
His hunting knife slicing Mike Alamo's calf,
Severing the artery, the blood spewing
All over the headliner of Crazy Horse,
My '55 Chevy, as we raced to save his life,
Tourniquetting with my belt.

Mike and Dante were friends. I arrived too late
To see why Dante drew the knife,
Why Mike tried to kick it out of his hand—
A combination of impatience and bravado
In our high school parking lot.

But I have since heard my share of crushed bones,
Of broken noses, jaws, and teeth;
I have seen and smelled my share of blood
All over walls, floors, ceilings,
Myself, my wife, as she tried to pull me off
The last man I sent to the hospital
With a shattered face.

Twenty thousand deaths a year from Road Rage.
Yet even Dante was sadistic,
Administering discipline and punishment
To foes whose only sin was envy,
Persecuting them forever in infernal fires.
Violence is very satisfying; it gratifies
Some primal urge. Denial.

Continued, no stanza break

Ignores millions of shaping eons.
Veterans of Project Phoenix came back
With not only ears, the equivalent of scalps,
But tales of pleasure they derived
From the sound of the knife along the neckbone.

Blood can feel good on your hands.
Slicing through the flesh of erstwhile friends
Provided even Dante with a rush.

Our Gang

The lug wrench hit Sam in the leg.
Their Midnight Auto gig seemed over,
But Michael pulled a gun and held it
To the owner's head and said,
"Finish the job," so Sam stripped it
Clean, man, while he smelled the shit
In the owner's pants and laughed.

Now Sam has an anklet
And he can't go anywhere
Without being monitored, dude,
Like perpetual surveillance
While he awaits his trial
Or bargains out on probation.

I saw his old lady drive by
And waved, but the dark glasses
Covered her swollen eyes
And her attempt at a smile
Dribbled down her chin
In a sob.

Stuck to her visor was a picture
Of Sam as a little boy
Trying things out on his first bike.
He graduated to a skateboard
And seemed as harmless
As a Norman Rockwell stereotype.

Sam wears dark glasses too
To cover the black eyes
His old man gave him.
One looks in vain for a sign of remorse,
Mouth flatlined into hateful defiance.

Because if he sings Mike says
He'll kill him,
So he takes the rap,
Favors his bum leg,
And waits to rejoin our gang.

Pedophilia Catholica

Where did you get that ring?
Do you like that? It's the mark of a secret society.
I'd like one. Do you want to join?
You'll have to undergo an initiation—
Something so secret, so private you'll never tell anyone.

Bless me, Father, for I have sinned —
He did what? One of our teachers?
He was dating my sister, you know, so I thought he was—straight.
You'll have to face him.
I don't know what he's talking about.
No, you wouldn't, you son-of-a-bitch.

They fired him, but I read in the paper,
When he got in the accident that almost killed him,
That he was teaching sixth grade in parochial school.
So the Church simply demoted him down from high to elementary,
From fifteen to twelve-year-old boys.
Now there's a model of good housekeeping.

The problem is systemic, built into a reciprocity
Of sado-masochism and single-sex environments.
The results are not accidental, they are predictable,
They are inescapable until the system itself is repudiated.

Meanwhile, the pain lasts, and it's sometimes the pain of guilt:
What did I do wrong? How could I have been so stupid?
So naïve? I must have been complicit.
But mostly it's the pain of betrayal:
How could he? How could they have let him?

If there were a god, s/he would protect at least the children.
Suffer them to come unto me.
Right. Through the grasping hands of pederasts.
Pain yields to anger. I hit him as hard as I could.
I wish he had died in the accident.

I wish there were a god to strike him dead before he does it again.
But there isn't. He hasn't even gone fishing.
He was never there to begin with,
Just a figment of our desire.

Desire. Like Buddha says, it gets us in a heap of trouble.
It even tricks us into thinking things are going to be ok
When they're not.
Desire is so trammeled up in denial.
Why don't we throw the bums out?
Because our psyches need them
And their perverse yet pleasing fictions.

Well, like Huck I may be damned to hell for heresy,
But you can count me out.
I'm taking a hammer and nails with me when I die,
And if He really exists after all,
I'm going to crucify Him.
Then I'll gladly go to hell,
Relieved to be shut of the whole sick mess.

Dark Night of the Soul

Busting fags in Lafayette Square
In the 50s was standard fare
For homophobes in high school in D.C.
But I didn't know when Phil and Ronnie
Invited us downtown one Friday night for fun.
"Lightnin'" and I giggled at the farce
Of scared men running from our gang,
Fleeing from the Marquis' monument.
I thought I heard him groaning underneath the ground.
But I did not experience the full shock of recognition
Till the sickening crush of fist on flesh and bone.
Phil's brass knuckles flashed in the hideous gleam of a streetlight.
And Ronnie kicked at the head of a fallen man with his combat boots.
At first at some deep level I enjoyed it
Because I had been molested,
But another, higher part of me revulsed.
Ashamed and scared I tried to leave
But Phil insisted with a hard twist of my arm
That I should stay, not spoil the fun.

He shoved me into the back of his Mercury,
And the scene shifted to Franklin Park,
The prey to "black fags," squealed pock-marked Ronnie.
Periph'rally, I saw the first resistant blade,
Whose flash distracted Phil and loosed his hold.
I grabbed Lightnin', and we split on a dead run.
A flashlight, a billy club, a military "Halt."
The bluecap marched us down 14th Street
Toward the paddy wagon's gaping maw.
"We've got them all" erupted from within.
"Sorry. Boys, you're free to go."
Turning the corner we sprinted to Phil's car,
Plunged in and gasped for air.
Abruptly, another flashlight shone upon
Our crotches as the silhouetted cap asked us
Mockingly, "What are you girls up to?"

Domestic Violence

"Say 'no thank you.'" "No tanks."
"Say 'no thank you.'" "No tanks."
So at her son's childish defiance
His mother took him hard by the arm
Away from the table and the staring faces
Because he'd embarrassed her
And slapped him
Hard
Again and again and again.

The boy lay in bed awake far into the night
Listening to the train whistles blow,
Vowing to run away,
To seek succor somewhere in the West,
But he fell asleep.

The next morning when he came down
His mother dropped the china cup
On the kitchen floor,
Staring horrified at his battered face.
She tried to say "I'm sorry,"
But in his family those words always stuck
In the craw.

His father held the boy's wrist
As he took off his belt
To give the boy a whipping
Like the one he'd given his brother
Across the dining room table.
So the boy bit his hand and ran away,
Hiding in the storm drain
Till he came home to find
His father was at confession,
Remorseful for what he did to his own son,

Continued, no stanza break

23

So the boy's mother said,
Though his father never said so
To him.

Then the boy grown man
Goes and knocks his oldest son's teeth out,
And takes a belt to his second son,
And slams a third up against the wall—
Even though he was finally in the West:
Go figure.

Ménage-à-trois

Grant's wife Linda brought men home that night.
One reached into her bra and cupped her breast
In front of him. Outraged I asked if he was going to hit him
Or was I. Grant broke his nose,
But he wanted to fight me,
Sir Galahad, who'd rescued Linda from their midst,
Sweeping her up from the bar and carrying her aloft
To her and Grant's own party for those of us
Whose fellowships were not renewed.
Already I had locked his friends in half-nelsons
And ground their faces in the carpet.

"Just take one step." He did. I felt his cheek-
bone crush beneath my fist, the rest a blur
Until I seemed to wake slowly, hearing far-off screams,
Feeling my throat being choked, someone on my shoulders:
Blood everywhere—ceiling, walls, furniture.
Blood on my arms and hands, my shirt ripped off,
And still the screaming from far off:
"Jesus, Doug, you're going to kill him!"
The arm around my neck my wife's, astride my back,
Her face covered with speckled blood.
All the bones in his face were shattered.
Grant grinned as they took him off.

At Crescent Beach in Florida Grant stood with a Schlitz.
He'd managed to stay at Hopkins somehow,
I'd moved on to Gator U.
"Mankind cannot afford one more euphoric," he mused
Of all the joints being rolled.
He had his daughter Laurie with him, Linda gone:
Vanished in pursuit of another hand
To cup her shattered being and make it whole.

Continued, no stanza break

Grant found another partner, seemed to find a modicum
Of happiness, till one day she showed up
With another man to get her clothes
And Grant got the gun and shot them both
Then shot himself.
She lives still on some funny farm,
Searching the horizon wistfully,
Hoping for yet another to make sense.

Grant is better off dead.
He would have hated fin de siècle:
Hippies turned to yuppies wearing nikes.
Ah, to die upon the edge before it dulls!
Pass me the carafe of wine,
Will you my dear? Where is the remote?

Professional Violence: The Agora

They're all so terribly bright
Sitting in the Hilton
Sipping their Scotch
Awaiting a call.
Furloughed from Siberian Snows
She glances at me furtively
Owl eyes darkly sunk.
Across the table my new Ph.D.
Chinks his ice, his fingers chewed,
Uninterviewed.
And my old friend mimics Momus:
Career, marriage, and himself undone.
Any one of them could have been —
Faces at tables laugh cavernous.
Human traffic twitches by
Nodding painful recognition.
Outside the city groans.
Recession humps the unemployed.
Israel humps Palestine.
North Korea flips the finger.
Saddam joins Elvis,
While they wounded sit wasting,
So terribly, terribly bright.

When Will They Ever Learn

You'd think the chiefs would learn,
From Chief Bull Connor to Chief Ed Davis
To Chief Botha to Chief Sharon,
That it's dangerous to make martyrs.
You know about all but Davis.
Let me tell you.

In the spring of 1970
When UCLA among myriad others
Was in an uproar over Cambodia
And Chief Rhodes's over-reaction
At Kent State,
Chief Davis's bulls invaded campus,
Closing it down by word of mouth.

From the top of Campbell Hall
It appeared *agents provocateurs*
Had succeeded in goading them
Into a charge.
Some threw stones, then retreated
Into the crowd of indignant
But unoffending students.
I found a burlap sack
Of pipes upon the roof,
Apparently deserted hastily.

I followed the horde into the library:
There the cops picked up a shelver
So abruptly, they broke both arms
Behind him.

Out near the Janss Steps
They spread-eagled Steve Yenser
And beat his balls into blue melons.
Over behind History they swarmed
At Peter Ladefoged because of the multi-colored shirt
African students had given him.

They beat this renowned Professor of Speech
Speechless,
Blood from their billyclubs
Clotting his thinning hair.

Then they turned on me, voyeur
Who'd seen too much,
And threw me down a stairwell,
Beating my back as I fell
Into fetal position—

Only to be reborn in the Senate,
Calling for the removal of ROTC,
Telling William French Smith at the Regents' meeting
That the real outside agitator was Richard Nixon,
The real violence precipitated by the government,
The National Guard, the LAPD—
The New Centurions enacting the New Rome.

The various Chiefs from Dulles to Davis
Had sacrificed hecatombs—
Ever since US broke our word to Ho Chi Minh
That if he helped US defeat the Japanese
We'd let him have his country.
Out of their ashes rose renewed resistance,
Till the real not the royal we
Finally brought one immoral war
To a dead
                    stand
                                    still.

So, Peter and Steve and that anonymous shelver:
This flower bud's for you.

Turkey Hunt

Steve filled the cup with white gas,
Tossed it on the just-lit kindling:
The resulting bonfire was typical of white men,
Not the Indians, but we were warm,
Settling into the White Mountains
The night before the turkey hunt.

"Twenty million here, twenty million there,
Our century's wars served as a prophylactic
Against overpopulation. What do we have to replace them?"
I'd never thought in those terms.
War was always bad even when it was good.
But here was a use of violence to consider.

I called and the turkeys answered
As early as four a.m.
They walked right through camp
As Steve made the coffee—
Too dark to see a damn thing.
So we glassed and glassed
When the sun came up
And finally spotted them
Down at the bottom of the meadow
Flush with mountain iris.

Steve hadn't fired his 30-30 in years
And it showed: he missed five times.
And I never got close enough with the shotgun.
So we spent the afternoon sighting in
Steve's old gun, the one for which he'd bought
The new firing pin right before we left Tucson.

The next morning we were waiting for them
Behind logs above the pond,
But I moved to get closer
And they spooked.
It was the last day of the hunt.

No stanza break

30

Steve went one way, I another,
When we met, he shrugged
And turned things over to me, the novice.
I thought returning to the scene of the crime
Was always a good idea.

There they were, we heard the clarion gobble
Even before we saw them in the meadow,
And Steve hurried to the top of the ridge,
Doffed his shooting-hand glove,
And shot that Tom through the neck
At seventy-five yards.

"So what predator will control
Our population explosion?" Steve asked,
As he gutted the gobbler.
"AIDS or staph," I replied;
"They can shoot even better than you,
Once they're sighted in."
"Ah, yes, trench mouth replaces trench warfare."
"And Ebola will make Hiroshima look like
A mere Antietam." "But the animal rightists
Want to stop us
Not only from hunting but fishing!
Jesus, what priorities.
Here, carry this rifle for me, will you?
I've got the bird." "Wait, let's take these feathers
Back to the shaman. He can use them."

That was a dozen or more years ago.
Steve's gone now, but a spring or two ago
I talked my first Tom right into my blind.
I didn't need a 30-30 (against the law now anyway):
My 12-gauge did just fine.
I thought what folly

Continued, no stanza break

Not to admit
That killing
Is endemic to our species.

With SARS now on the scene,
Will the turkeys not outlive us?

For Nicole Brown Simpson

Not since Sharon Tate—
What she must have suffered!
Grotesque as in a Faulkner novel,
Blade against the neckbone.

The dangling heads of Tutsis.

Various Voices
of Violence

Rape's Revenge

Black circles under grey Crotty eyes,
Broken shoulder healed, broken jaw,
But not broken hymen, broken heart.

Twice the jury hung, twice his parents lied.
We swore a pact 'mong brothers if we ever catch him:
To cut off his dick, douse it, make him smoke it;
Disembowel him with my hunting knife;
Dig out each eye so the last thing he sees is her,
In person or in picture, whichever she prefers.

Then rip his heart out beating,
Each of us taking a bite.

Don Juan

Nothing quite like it:
The thrill of taking
The wife, the daughter
Of the Superego,
My cousin, my sister,
My best friend's mother—

Heart pounding not just with passion
But fear, for He sleeps in the room
Next door—

Heart still pounding,
Lying spent trying
To silence my breathing,
Listening to her as she creeps
In alongside him,
Envisioning her beautiful derrière
On the edge of his bed
Curved away from him towards my
Still tumescent phallus—

My *défiance* of his *affiance*.
I welcome the *desafío*.

Doc

You all right, Doc?
Here, let me lick the blood
From the corners of your mouth.

I saw you wink at Billy Clanton
So your gun and not Virgil's stick
Would rule the day.

Here, let me kiss those hieratic hands,
The instruments of sacrifice.

The doctor says you're dying, Doc,
But what a way to go.

Here, let me suck the tip of your gun
And drain the rush from it.

Shootout

The balls of his feet are sore from the boots,
The inside of his thighs from the saddle;
Salt stains are visible on his shirt,
And his beard is choked with dust.

The clouds are bleeding orange to red.
He cocks his Colt to check,
Spins the cylinder, lowers the hammer,
And sheathes it back in his holster.

The cosmos emptying of light
Whispers nothings in his ear.
He waits for his formidable adversary
To emerge from the lighted saloon,

Thinking to himself, only this is real,
This moment on the edge
Of being or of nothingness,
Of quick or dead meat.

A silhouette darkens the doorway,
Coat behind the gun.
Both hands reach at once,
Both guns roar.

Knocked off his horse on his butt
By the impact on his shoulder,
He grits the pain, remounts, and rides off,
His father shot through the heart.

Geronimo Speaks

Crook says I have killed people, settlers,
But it was war, bad things happen in war.
Nantan Lupan says I have killed women and children,
But so has the White-Eye.

For centuries the bearded conquerors
Have killed, captured, enslaved us.
We have engaged them in total war;
We have tried to kill them all.

For they are the invaders,
And the only way to stop them
From taking our land
Is to annihilate them.

If we lose, we will not be the first
People to be exterminated by the march
Of some other people's manifest destiny,
Nor will we be the last.

Let the White-Eye beware.
His America may be the new Rome,
Laying its foundations
On the blood of the conquered.

Rome fell, exhausted
Like a spent elk
Harried by invaders.
Yesterday's barbarians are tomorrow's Diné.

The Dreamer says our chiefs will return
That we may wrest the land back from the White-Eye—
Or will it be other Asian warriors,
Both our ancestors and our descendents at once?

Chato's Lament

It is not that we never raided
Before the Europeans came;
It is not that we never took captives:
We adopted them into our tribes.

But since the Bearded-ones' advent,
Our women and little children
Are captured, bought and sold,
Working their homes, their fields, their mines.

We have learned from them that they
Will buy any slave, Indian or Mexican.
So we have traded in slaves with the white men.
And now I want to make trade.

My family is not on my farm at Turkey Creek.
My family is on a rancho in Chihuahua.
I ask the Great White Father
To get them back for me.

Our mothers know the pangs of childbirth;
Our fathers know the pride of sons
Successfully completing vision quests,
Of daughters marrying chiefs.

We know the tug of tears and laughter
Just like you. Our "savagery"
Has room for compassion and sacrifice
And honor.

Where is the honor of the European?
Is it only in the books
They write to brainwash their children?
Or in the empty words of their treaties?

You have given me a blank piece of paper.
You have given me a shining medal
Made of the silver we have been enslaved
To mine for you, signifying nothing.

You have stripped me of my commission as scout.
You have detained me at Fort Leavenworth
As a "prisoner of war." Will I never see
The land of the Diné again?

It appears I must join Geronimo
In Florida to waste away
The rest of my warrior's life:
May I at least be imprisoned with my family?

Ballads from Hell
(Myself Am Hell)

The Sisyphus Rock

Get up, Sisyphus, get up.
Pick up that stone, get up.
For the home team's sake, pick it up.
You don't know for certain that it's all in vain;
You must negotiate the hill again:
Persevere, Old Reprobate, pick up that rock —
Get up, Sisyphus, get up.

There's rioting in the streets:
A labyrinth of defeats;
Whole histories of retreats.
Despite our propensity to kill the King,
Though hatred won't let freedom ring,
Pick it up, Old Sinner, interdict Fell Night —
Get up, Sisyphus, get up.

There seems no end to war:
Towns burn just as before;
Astraea proves a whore.
Despite our incompetence to keep the peace,
Though chaos threatens us from west to east,
Keep it up, Old Climber, contradict thy curse —
Get up, Sisyphus, get up.

There's never enough to eat;
Refugees still gash their feet:
Our world is incomplete.
Though man's frustration seems permanent,
Though despair cries unanswered to the firmament,
Yet arise, Old Timer, in defiance strive —
Get up, Sisyphus, get up.
Pick up that stone, get up.

Continued, no stanza break

For all our sake, pick it up.
You don't know for certain that it's all in vain;
You must negotiate the hill again.
Persevere, Old Reprobate, pick up that rock —
Get up, Sisyphus, get up.

1968

Hang On, Ixion

Hang on, Ixion, and take another spin.
Hang on, Ixion, and sing the fall of kings:
Who's up and who's down, who's out and who's in—
Hang on, Ixi, take the cyclic view of things.

Sing of great Hector, who sealed the fate of Troy:
Against his better judgment, he yielded to a boy;
Chary of his "honor" and wary of "disgrace,"
He fought for a whore just "to save his country's face."

Great Caesar fought with Pompey, Marc Antony with his son,
Balance of power failed, alliance was undone:
And thus colossi strive in slaughter fabulous—
"This world just isn't big enough for both of us."

King Lear, like Oedipus and a thousand more beside,
Had a great fall because of great pride,
Which wouldn't be so bad, but like the wheel you're on,
When they run downhill, they drag the world along.

We ever have our Crusades fought in the name of Truth,
And for our holy wars we do gladly give our youth:
For Jesus or for Luther, for Allah or for God,
We send our countless millions to lie beneath the sod.

Some say it's man's aggression that makes him act this way,
Some say his fallen nature, come down from Adam's day,
But whether he fights for Marx or for democracy,
There's no killer in this world quite like ideology.

You'd think Hitler would learn from Napoleon's defeat
That you don't invade a country whose climate can't be beat;
You'd think he'd learn from Pilate that you don't kill Jews—
But then you'd think we'd learn from him dictators to refuse.

Continued, no stanza break

We've with our modern temper no Dispenser of the Rings,
But we have our Kennedys and our Martin Luther Kings:
They earn the fate of Gandhi and that of Jesus Christ—
Since Socrates our gadflies are ever sacrificed.

So we turn to revolution, mob rule rears its bloody hand:
Mere anarchy is loosed upon the land,
Followed by a Reign of Terror and a brand new elite—
Such corps of impudent snobs are anything but effete.

Be it king or common man, the fate is still the same,
Whether reaching for the skies or a lower, humbler aim:
Seduced by his dreams, betrayed by his desire,
Man ends up bound forever on a wheel of fire.

Hang on, Ixion, and take another spin.
Hang on, Ixion, and sing the fall of kings:
Who's up and who's down, who's out and who's in—
And let us take upon ourselves the mystery of things.

1970

Chin Up, Tantalus

Chin up, Tantalus, keep a stiff upper lip,
Don't let your frustrations get you down;
Though the object of your reach is giving you the slip,
Keep your hands to yourself and don't grovel on the ground.

Though your children are all cutups, yet we know they're good at heart.
Don't let their silly antics be cause for your alarm:
Though they get on each others' *wives* and they probe each other's smart,
That they rue what they do proves they mean no body harm.

See, it's for the country's good that Queen Helen proves a whore,
And it's for the army's good that Iphigenie must be killed:
For your countrymen unite and they fight a glorious war—
What matter how they win or how much blood is spilled?

So Agamemnon must die, you can't have everything,
And the cycle must go on for the good of the race,
For as everyone knows, we must kill the king—
That the seasons may change we must bear some disgrace.

So Niobe sheds her kids and Orestes kills his mother—
It happens in the best of families!
Besides Orestes gets off, Pelops pulls himself together,
And Helen comes home to cure her husband's disease.

So chin up, Tantalus, it's not all that bad,
See how evil ever turns into good:
Though your curse still persists and the world runs mad,
We yet uphold the tradition of brotherhood.

1970

The Prometheus Stone
(a galling sequel to The Sisyphus Rock)

Eat your heart out, Prometheus,
You may have been wrong
To ever let men play with fire.

Sure, it helps them keep snug,
But as the chimneys belch smoke
And the cars cough smog
And the sky spits soot,
As the forest fires rage
And the oil wells blaze,
Is there a gnawing in your gut
That you did the wrong thing?

Eat your heart out, Prometheus,
You may have been rash
To ever let men play with fire.

Sure, it helps them forge on,
But as the booby traps blow
And the bombs explode
And the bullets lay low,
As the napalm spreads jelly
And the mushroom spreads clouds,
Is there a sinking in your tummy
That you did the wrong thing?

Eat your heart out, Prometheus,
You may have been negligent
To ever let men play with fire.

Sure, it helps illuminate,
But as the cities ignite
And the libraries burn
And the crops are laid waste,
As unbelievers light torches

Continued, no stanza break

And the ovens cook Jews,
Is there a visceral urging
That you did the wrong thing?

Eat your heart out, Prometheus,
You may have been improvident
To ever let men play,
To ever let men play,
To ever let men play with fire.

1971

Don't You Feel Like a Heel, Achilles

Don't you feel like a heel, Achilles,
For having prolonged the war?
It would have been so nice
If you had followed their advice
To have ended it all in one big roar.

But then you didn't have plutonium,
Didn't even have uranium,
Had only your sword
To back up your word
And its ability to stab or split asunder a cranium.

How's it look to you now, Achilles,
Now we have the ultimate tool?
Should pride stand in our way,
Should there be more to say
Before reducing the earth t'another primordial pool?

1972/2000

Recent Thunderings and Whisperings

Terrorism

No image can replace the one burned into our retinae:
The second plane, the crumbling towers, the plummeting refugees.

One tries to articulate the unspeakable in the last century:
From Armenia to Hitler's Germany to Stalin's Russia
To Hiroshima, My Lai, Cambodia, El Mozote.
Donde están los desaparecidos?

But suicide bombers are different,
Bred by desperation, facing superior power,
From Ireland to Palestine
They strike out, dismembering.

Parts of bodies slap us in the face,
And we retaliate with tanks and missiles,
Carpet bombing, fire bombing,
Masking in revenge the causes.

And now my generation
Has gone from dropping daisies into rifle barrels
To dropping daisy cutters from the sky.

Because who can brook a slap in the face?
Who has the time to ferret out reasons?
To hesitate is positively unpatriotic.

Men of the Millenium

Surely Martin Luther for delivering
Us from Romish, papal tyranny,
Madison for the Establishment Clause
Delivering us from tyranny of religion,

In whose name so many nameless horrors
Have been committed just by Europeans
In their missionary zeal t'extend
Their cultural hegemony round the world.

Not to mention Islamic jihad
For more than a millenium and a half
From Mecca to Malaysia and Madrid
To Taliban in poor Afghanistan.

But these two world religions have no claim
T'exclusive rights of mental slavery.
From rabbis to witch doctors, shamans—priests
Of every cult all bear collective guilt

Of persecution based on superstition,
Denial of human rights, especially women's
And children's, both sometimes consigned
To other forms of slavery, often sex.

All in the name of Jesus or of Allah
Or of Vishnu or Jehovah, even
Buddha, in spite of ideology
Of peace and love—both masks of irony.

Madison and Luther must be rolling over
In their graves, each staggered by the concept
Of a moral majority denying human rights
Or establishing religion in a state.

Each must be muttering this simple prayer:
"Some Power save me from theocracy."

D. C. Revisited

Coming up 15th Street, Northwest, approaching H,
I began to recognize before knowing remembered:
It's whiter now than it was fifty years ago,
Probably sand-blasted,
But the bricks above the stone are still
Corrugated yellow-brown, like Notre Dame bricks —
The Woodward Building.

Hotel Sofitel is now catty-cornered to it.
After checking in, I dropped down to the bar
To wait for Chris, and there it was again,
Outside the plate-glass windows,
Squatting tri-cornered, as it were,
Magisterial in its serene solidity,
Like Napoleon's Tomb.

I remembered: the L4 downtown after school
To the dentist's office, that sadist's den,
Then holding my jaw, I'd make my way
From K on down to H
And Dad's law offices on the sixth floor,
Where I'd wait for him, talking to Suzie,
Till he emerged doublebreasted,

His American Legion pin in his lapel,
Not for service in the second but the first
World War as a drill instructor:
I'd seen his sergeant's stripes.
He rarely had the car, so we'd take the trolley,
Then the bus to Chevy Chase Circle,
The fountain teasing my thoughts skyward.

Continued, stanza break

If we ever talked on those trips home,
I don't remember. I just recall
His wrinkled raincoat o'er his arm,
His frumpled hat.
He read the paper mostly,
The *News* and not the *Post* or *Star* (too pink).
I'd read my homework or just stare.

The one time he seemed to care
Was when he made me watch
The Army-McCarthy hearings
After school.
He wanted me to understand the danger
Of fifth-column commies in our midst.
He died before I understood the threat.
But then I understood it upside down.
Now here I was in town to read proposals
In cultural history that would deconstruct
My father's world.

So my nostalgia kept bouncing off
The stolidity of that old building
Even as catty-cornered across Lafayette Square
The New McCarthyites
Plotted assaults on the Bill of Rights.

Chris showed up just in time
To save me from my ruminations.
We downed a scotch together,
Then ambled off
Down 15th Street past the Woodward
To rooftop terrace dining,

Whence I could see a savage thunderstorm approach,
Threatening the Jefferson, the Lincoln, the Washington itself,
Obdurate obelisk amidst the rolling clouds
And electrifying lightning—
As if it stood for something durable.

After many a beer, much cheer, we ambled back,
And I paused to marvel at the marble face
Of Old Woodward.
I thought I heard my father "Hmmph"
And looked aloft to his old office —
Nothing there but brick.

Les Oiseaux du printemps

I could always whistle like a bird.
In eighth grade Sister Gonzaga searched
For him in the closet. And in French
Class at Notre Dame my friend DuBois
Announced spring's advent in the midst of winter,
For *"Les oiseaux du printemps chantent déjà."*

Indeed. The recent photograph shows Bob
DuBois has aged, divorced again, the lines
Lengthening down his handsome face, drawing
His smile down in scorn at turning sixty,
Yet he asked, *"Si les oiseaux du printemps
Chantent encore?"* Good question, Monsieur Bob.

Sure they do, but do they sing for us?
We fought for civil rights, and yet the headline
Yesterday reported blacks pay more
For mortgages. We fought against the war,
But now a friend prepares the paratroops
For the imminent attack upon Iraq.

Do they sing for America? where aging
Citizens can't get prescriptions filled
Because Congress cowers before the rich
And won't raise taxes social programs need?
Where every sixteen minutes someone dies
Awaiting transplant for a lack of donors?

Do they sing for an overcrowded planet?
Do they sing for twenty million AIDS
Victims in Africa alone? Do they
Sing eternal return? Or do they mark,
Like the canaries in the mines, our im-
              minent demise?

On Tampa Bay
(at a Conference for Cultural Studies)

Over Tampa harbor inlets pelicans float,
Searching for their own fish breakfast
To match the salmon I am eating
On a bagel, complete with capers,
As I watch through the window of the Wyndham,
Which, like its neighbor monoliths, perches
On the shores, brooding.

I too brood: on whose backs this luxury?
Rosania called from Room Service to say
Breakfast was on its way up. The cabby
Was from Tunisia, spoke mellifluous Arabic
To his sweetheart on his cellphone.
The wizened black who wheeled me from the plane
Was from Jamaica, glowed with pleasure
When I told him that my oldest son
Was a professor of Caribbean literature.

Last month, as always in D.C.,
The waitress was an Ethiopian as beautiful
As Black Venus must have been.
The cabbies hailed from Ghana, Eritrea,
And everywhere the dulcet tones of Spanish.
The Cambodians ran the doughnut shop;
The lady from the PRC sold me the T-shirt.

Is this the meaning of global? the appropriation
Of a service class? Even the leftist professors,
Like me here for the conference,
Luxuriate in the comfort they provide
At a wage so minimum
It's to airy thinness beat.

Continued

Overhead rattles by the helicopter.
I know it's to watch the morning traffic,
But it connotes surveillance:
Can't be too safe in Ashcroft's Amerika.

The sun struggles with the clouds for dominance.
It will lose. The pelicans themselves
Have given up. And I have eaten my fill.
Time to listen to Anglo academics
Talk about cultural studies.

Out West

Like multitudes before me
I went west, ignorant of Greeley,
Lummis, a schoolboy's acquaintance
With Lewis, Clark, Parkman, Carson, Frémont.
Cummings had captured Buffalo Bill forever,
And tv had made Hollywood's west available,
From Tom Mix and Bob Steele to Ken and Kermit Maynard,
Roy and Gene and Hoppy, Lone Ranger, Tonto.
I went west with Wayne and Stewart, *Broken Arrow, Shane*:
Jack Palance as Wilson, "Prove it," then again as Torreano:
Heston broke his back. (Symbolic? Nah.
No more than the meaning of Tonto's name
Nor the vanishing of Senseearay,
Plowed, seeded, dead;
White-Eyes ride overhead.)
College kids crowded tv rooms to watch *Maverick*,
Cheyenne, Bronco, Sugarfoot, Lawman, Rifleman.
I was ambushed as we cut south from the Platte toward Denver.

There they were, rising, looming, purple shades,
A silhouette on the horizon, rotating toward me
As if I were the first. And I was simply awed.
From out of the past came the thundering hoofbeats of
The Rockies.

What did it mean, the West?
The Frontier—latecomer Anglos finally there to conquer,
To possess, to make it part of *our* Manifest Destiny.
Embodied first in the Mountain Men
Then the explorers, homesteaders, cattlemen.
Then in the Rough Riders, speak softly, big stick,
Cowboy-gunboat diplomacy,
Yankee derring-do.
All the way to Iwo, firing from the hip.

Now in here, inside Americans,
Part of our national character.
Nourishing our Roman urge,

Continued, no stanza break

The New Frontier and American Adventurism,
Vietnam and Cuba and see who blinks first.
Kissinger to Fallacci called himself Lone Ranger.
Holmes Tuttle said, "Get us a cowboy,"
And Ronnie rode out of the West
To take the govmint back from effete snobs
And pynty-headed intyllectuls,
Take our destiny back from
Bead-wearing, pot-smoking, hirsute hippies:
God save us from political correctness!

Armed with the doctrine of preemption,
Out of Texas rides Lone Shrub,
Wearing headphones whence emanates
The voice of Whispering Cheney,
"Shoot now, questions later,
And those you won't have to answer."

Can't think about it all without falling
Into stereotype and caricature.
Funny how life imitates art.
"Fastest draw in the West —
Want to see it again, Saadam?"
What is obscured is the source
Of all the fireworks,
Lurking underneath
In primeval pools.
Like the gold and silver and copper
Running through the veins
Of Gaia, Goddess of the Earth
We must possess
Before
Someone else does,
Unworthy,
Unhouseled,
Unannealed—
Un-American.

The Shadow Knows

At Peace

A recorder modulates through a baroque concerto
The rising sun causes the morning clouds to blush
I sit at the patio table nursing a cup of coffee
Grateful to the cosmos for vouchsafing me another day

My lungs crackle as I breathe
Reminding me of my deadly passenger
My wife fights with one son in the kitchen
Another son fights with his wife in the bedroom

I sip my coffee thinking of terrorists
Thinking of anger and violence
Regretting my own inflictions
Smiling, toasting *élan vital*

As it hurls us toward other suns

Stowaway
(in anticipation of a transplant that never came)

Lurking in my lungs
I know you're there
I don't mind giving you a lift
Even though you're deadly

I do not fear you
You're just a part of life
A nasty part for egotists
Who think the world cannot do without them

So if it's all the same with you
I'm going to drop you at the nearest port
And take on a working swabbie
Who'll help me sail the seven seas

A few years longer
Perhaps a decade or two
In the South Seas
That would be capital

Perhaps I'll achieve something immortal
                Perhaps not

For Taylor

Taylor Blake, the teenager with brain
Tumor inoperable, said if she died
Earlier than she'd like to, it's ok.
She did, and no, it's not ok with me.
Beauty, youth, vitality, aplomb—
Wasted. I hope nobody prays.

They want to pray for me, have masses said.
I tell them it's liable to backfire.
Better watch out, for I'm a lightning rod.
Don't stand too close. Like Ahab I hang on,
Saying through gritted teeth *I can be ashes*.
But then my ashes won't be young and warm.

Who Needs Kavorkian

I can always eat a bullet:
Cold steel of the barrel in my mouth,
The blast splattering my brains out
Over my study wall.

Or maybe there ought to be more ritual,
Like disembowelment,
Slumping over my entrails
In ultimate abjection.

Or playing Russian roulette
With the Blackhawk,
Spinning the cylinder,
Eyeing the Reaper in the mirror.

Screw you, Shadow! You don't know Jack Shit.

Or maybe something more soothing,
A drive up to the mountains,
A walk at high altitudes,
A sleep underneath a pine.

Good night, sweet prince.

Above all, avoid self-pity.
Just void the self. Your self.
Don't become a suffocating object
Of others' pity.

But soft, the fair Ophelia —

The New Haven Green
(fall 1963)

Silhouettes against a blushing sun,
Silhouettes against the motley leaves,
They loll, the old ones, ruminating.

Put out to pasture now,
They low in parks;
They give us no more milk;

And we refuse
To suck the wisdom from their withering minds
Before it curds.

Silhouettes 'gainst gashed vermillion's glory,
These shadows of mankind evaporate.

The Medium Is the Message

L. D.'s last story is about air.
How appropriate.
Air is indeed the medium of our tribe,
Our most precious commodity.

How fresh the air must have been
When the Apaches breathed it
In the mountains we have hunted since,
Cresting breathless another ridge,

Surrounded by manzanita
Or by ponderosa,
The huge canopy of sky
Streaked with cirrus.

No smelters then,
Belching sulfur,
No interstates
Exhausting the land.

Not to mention city smog
Or the chemicals that kill insidiously,
Interstitially,
Idiopathically.

But there's no global warming,
No cause for alarm
From the burning
Of the rain forest.

So breathe a sigh of relief,
Fellow tribesmen.
All's well
In Middle-Earth.

The corporate
Prince of Air
Has replaced the old one
With global benevolence,

And I am dumb to tell . . .

Aurora

The morning chill slipped a hand
Underneath my sweatshirt,
And the Gibbous moon hung aloft
Pendant in ambiguity,

While the quail cock chocked his dominion
Against the sky and the dove
Fluttered out in front of me
Unflappable.

I scooped up the paper,
Full of the latest violations,
And held the loose end of the plastic bag
Like a dead squirrel's tail,

Content with suspending
My re-engagement in world events
Awhile, attendant instead
To the bluing around me,

The lighting of the eastern sky,
Licking with hints of vermillion
The dissipating clouds
And I, lapped in wonder.

Florence

I love a nurse. Hell, I married one.
And I've had some since that knocked my socks off:
"Alice" the Asian, Barbara the Chicana, Tanya the African-American,
Each of whom shared my—it wasn't pain, not even anxiety—
                                    My lust for breath.

Gray specters moving slowly down halls,
Clinging to life while IV's cling to them:
It's a tunnel vision that can overwhelm
And so as much as I respond to my nurse's touch
                                    I take my mind away.

On my dresser are photos of the nurse I married,
Each one with eyes redolent of the force
That drove her green age and now drives our gray.
I follow their gaze past corridors of decay
                                    Toward the light,

Toward the boughs where still the sweet birds sing.
My Florence is indeed a nightingale.
We walk Firenze's streets quietly after dark;
She nurses my breathing back to life,
                                    To the sublime.

Past the house of Dante's birth, nestled in the shadows,
Past the Palazzo Vecchio, rising in the artificial light,
Towards the Duomo, brooding o'er the vast abyss
Peopled with aspiration, inspiration:
                                    I share her sigh.

Je veux dire

I will to say what words themselves can't say:
I will t'articulate my love for you.
Characterize my feelings' disarray
Is something that escapes my will to do.

For love is nothing facile to describe,
Imperfect signifiers all to use.
Yet love is feeling deep, too deep to hide,
And thus my words to you will bring no news.

My eyes alone can tell the depth of love
And them by means we humans cannot know.
For love is cosmic gravity, above
Our wills, manifest in an inner glow.

Look deep, therefore, into my inmost heart,
And see there signs we nevermore shall part.

The North Oregon Coast, Summer '02

Where the finite meets the infinite:

The crab, gull-bait, scurries at the edge of the foam;
The bull elephant-seal mounts his tawny mate,
And she lolls on the rocks for days, gestating;

Cormorants stretch their necks while flying swift and low;
Two grey whales cavort, raising their backs above their element,
Like Antony and Cleopatra, oblivious to our gaze.

Two kites are fingered expertly aloft, twinkling in their medium;
The lighthouse harvests its beams for night outbursts,
Standing abject sentinel above the cosmic undulations.

We walk the strand at low tide and get as close as we can
To the sunning seal pups, dotting the spit in dollops of fur.
We stand reverent in the windy hush, as a monitor apparently eyes us
      askance.

My sons, their wives; my wife, and I: one tide ebbing, the other coming in,
Suspended in the fold between,
Where the finite meets the infinite,

Toujours déjà

Breathless

Not like a nun, though in adoration
Of the gashed embers of an Arizona sunset,
In awe of the self-sacrifice of the FDNY
And *les médecins sans frontières*.
Nature's glory, human glory—

Little things that take your breath away:
The bridal bouquets of white
Atop the mighty saguaros, spite of drought;
The mist rising from surf exploding on Pacific rocks;
The exceeding green carpets of Irish plains and Welsh mountains;
Korean and Japanese children holding hands with players in the
        World Cup;
The Aztec lurking in the face of the Mexican athlete;
A mountain gorilla peeling leaves off a twig through his teeth;
Baboons lining the highway for miles in a funeral procession;
Young adults demolishing the Berlin Wall with sledge hammers;
Jackie in her blood-stained suit holding the bible for Lyndon's oath;
Wizened Mandela emerging from prison smiling;
The lone Chinese student facing down a tank;
A peregrine falcon stooping with unbelievable speed;
Technicolor images of our sister planets, their moons,
Our own blue earth, veiled with wispy white;
The pregnant wife of a mutilated Phoenix policeman:
They celebrate new life amidst grotesquerie.

                Awesome, dude.
                Ad majoram daily gloriam.

Epilogue

Barry Bonds's 73rd

The gods don't have a monopoly
On the sacred, you know.
Spartacus touched it in the valleys
Of Calabria; Ghandi touched it
In the Valley of the Indus;
Mandela touched it in the blackest prison;
Einstein touched it on the perihelion of Mercury,
Suu Kyi on the backroads of Burma,
Mother Jones in the tents of Colorado
Before the Rockefeller Pinkertons opened fire
With those wonderful new
Fire-breathing dragons called machine guns.

And sometimes athletes have touched it in their way:
Jim Thorpe, the tri-, penta-, deka-, mega-athlete of his day,
The two Babes and Ben and Tarzan himself.
Jesse Owens touched it as he streaked
By Hitler's youth, and FloJo, streaking toward a rendezvous
With early death, but today
Barry Bonds touched it at the end of a bat:
A secular violence that constitutes
A sacred achievement in the name of all of us,
For it extends our capacity to be

                    Free

From the limits the gods would impose on us—
A capacity born of blood and meat
And linked to the ancient lynxes
That stalked the beating hearts of the night.

About the Author (1941-2003)

Douglas Canfield died July 3, 2003 after a long and valiant battle with idiopathic pulmonary fibrosis, relinquishing his being to the cosmos whence it sprang.

He was the author of several scholarly books and articles in the two fields of Restoration and early eighteenth-century British Literature (particularly the drama) and comparative literature and culture of the Southwest borderlands. In the spring of 2001, he was invited to Italy, to the University of Florence to lecture in this latter field and to the university of Tuscia to lecture in the former, where a series translations of Restoration comedies into Italian has begun in his honor.

Canfield won several fellowships for his scholarship, the most recent from the National endowment for the Humanities in 2000-2001. He was also the winner of several teaching awards, including 1993 Arizona Professor of the Year. .

Dr. Canfield was committed to social justice, and his favorite course to teach was "The Ideology of Human Rights," and his dying wish was for world peace with justice as he descended "down to darkness on extended wings," believing along with his favorite poet, Wallace Stevens, that "death is the mother of beauty."

His poetry collection, *The Graying of the Sixties*, was published by Burning Cities Press in 2002.

www.ingramcontent.com/pod-product-compliance
Lightning Source LLC
Chambersburg PA
CBHW072154020426

42334CB00018B/2002